There are five titles in the 'Get Going With Creative Writing' series:

All About Me – 978-1-907733-90-1

Likes and Dislikes – 978-1-907733-91-8

Out and About – 978-1-907733-92-5

We Love Animals – 978-1-907733-93-2

What We Do – 978-1-907733-94-9

Guinea Pig Education
2 Cobs Way
New Haw, Addlestone
Surrey
KT15 3AF
Tel: 01932 336553
Website: www.guineapigeducation.co.uk

© Copyright 2014

NO part of this publication may be reproduced, stored or copied for commercial purposes and profit without the prior written permission of the publishers.

ISBN: 978-1-907733-90-1

Written: Sally A Jones and Amanda C Jones
Illustrations: Sally A Jones
Graphic Design: Annalisa Jones
USA Editing: S. Waller

Dear Kids,

Have fun learning to write with our 'Get Going With Creative Writing' series. Enjoy reading our short stories; some which have been written by kids of your age. Use our ideas to write your own stories, or try some non-fiction writing, such as, diaries, reports and leaflets. If you read or write well you will achieve high grades at school, so we challenge you to learn to love writing. You just need a notebook and pencil to start working through your guinea pig writing guide. Don't forget to color in the pictures.

....

Dear Teachers and Parents,

If your children think writing is dull, give them a guinea pig writing book from the 'Get Going With Creative Writing' series and we think they'll change their minds. However, these books are also ideal for those children who love to write, providing starting points that will make any budding young writer's imagination run wild, especially if they are preparing for standardized tests.

We have put together a series of themed books to inspire your child to write at his or her level. Whether you choose 'About Me,' 'We Love Animals,' 'Likes and Dislikes,' 'Out And About' or 'What We Do,' you will choose an English study book with a light-hearted, modern approach to appeal to the children of today.

The books can be used at home or in school alongside the existing curriculum. Inside, you will find a treasure trove of ideas for writing, featuring fiction and non-fiction themes. Based on the National Curriculum in the UK, they comply with respected strategies for literacy, with tips on planning and writing techniques, sentence construction, grammar tips and more.

Written by a former teacher, working as a tutor, the books have been tested by the children the author teaches in Surrey, England. These children agree the books are fun and help them learn to love writing.

> **We would like to thank the students of Guinea Pig Tuition – class of 2010/2011 – Sophia, Georgina, Harriet, Hannah, Sacha, Harry, Gareth, Rahan, Neena, Mahir, Neesha, Jai, Alexandra, Anna Maria and Vlad.**

First things first...

Sam's rabbit says, "Can you write your name, address and phone number?"

Write your best friend's address, his or her house number, street, town, and phone number.
Make an address book.

Sam says, "I can help you write <u>interesting sentences</u>."

<u>Do not</u> use the same word to start a sentence:

- I am short.
- I have brown hair.
- I wear a striped t-shirt.

<u>Join your ideas</u> using conjunctions like:

- and
- but
- because
- so
- who *(to describe people)*
- which *(to describe things)*

I am short and I have brown hair, so I wear a striped t-shirt.

Use **<u>good words</u>**.

Read some information about Sam.

He writes in the first person (I).

Sam is my name and I am eight years old. There are four people in my family who are Mom, Dad, my sister Kim and me.

I am a small boy and I have short brown hair with sparkling blue eyes. The clothes I like to wear are a pair of old blue jeans and a striped t-shirt.

Since I enjoy sports, I am very active. My teacher says I talk too much and must learn to work quietly.

Grammar Tip

A conjunction joins ideas in a sentence. These words are also conjunctions: after, as, while, although, for, until, if, when, since, unless, or, where and whether. Use them to join ideas together. The words 'who' and 'which' are pronouns, but they can also be used to join ideas together.

Read about Kim.

Sam writes in the third person *(he, she, it, they).*

Sam says,

"Kim is very tall and she has has long dark hair which she ties back in buns. She has rosy red lips and bright green eyes.

Her favorite dress is a patterned tunic which she wears with skinny jeans and flip flops.

When she is with her friends, Kim is always sweet and kind, but she often teases me and gets me into trouble with Mom and Dad. After school, she plays with our cat Molly because she loves animals."

Write about Sam.

Sam is ..eight.... years old. In his family he has .... and .... The name of his sister is .... He is .... with .... hair and .... eyes. His favorite clothes are a .... At school he enjoys ...., but his teacher says he ....

Write about Kim.

Kim is .... Her hair is .... and .... She has .... lips and .... eyes. The dress she likes best is a .... At school she is .... when she is with her friends, but she .... her brother Sam. After school, she loves to ....

Your turn to write...

Think about the answers to these questions. Use the questions to help you.

- **What is your name?**

  My name is ....

- **How old are you?**

  I am .... years old.

- **How many people are there in your family?**

  In my family there are ....

- **Do you have any brothers or sisters?**

  The name of my .... is/are ....
  ....

- **What do you look like?**

  As for me, I have .... eyes and .... hair.

- **Are you tall or short?**

  For my age, I am ....

- **What is your character like?**

  When I am at home, I am ....
  When I am at school, I am ....
  ....

> Describe another member of your family in three sentences.

What are his or her eyes like?

blue	bright	green	shiny
sad	brown	sparkling	hazel
grey			

What is his or her hair like?

blonde	light	shiny	brown
dark	black	chestnut	grey
white	curly	straight	frizzy
long	short	medium length	in a bob
braided	french-braided	in a ponytail	in a bun

What do they look like?

tall	short	small	huge
giant	fat	thin	slim
overweight	well built	underweight	pretty
ugly	handsome	young	old

Example:

Grandad is very short and well built. His hair is long, grey and curly. He has bright blue eyes that make him look happy.

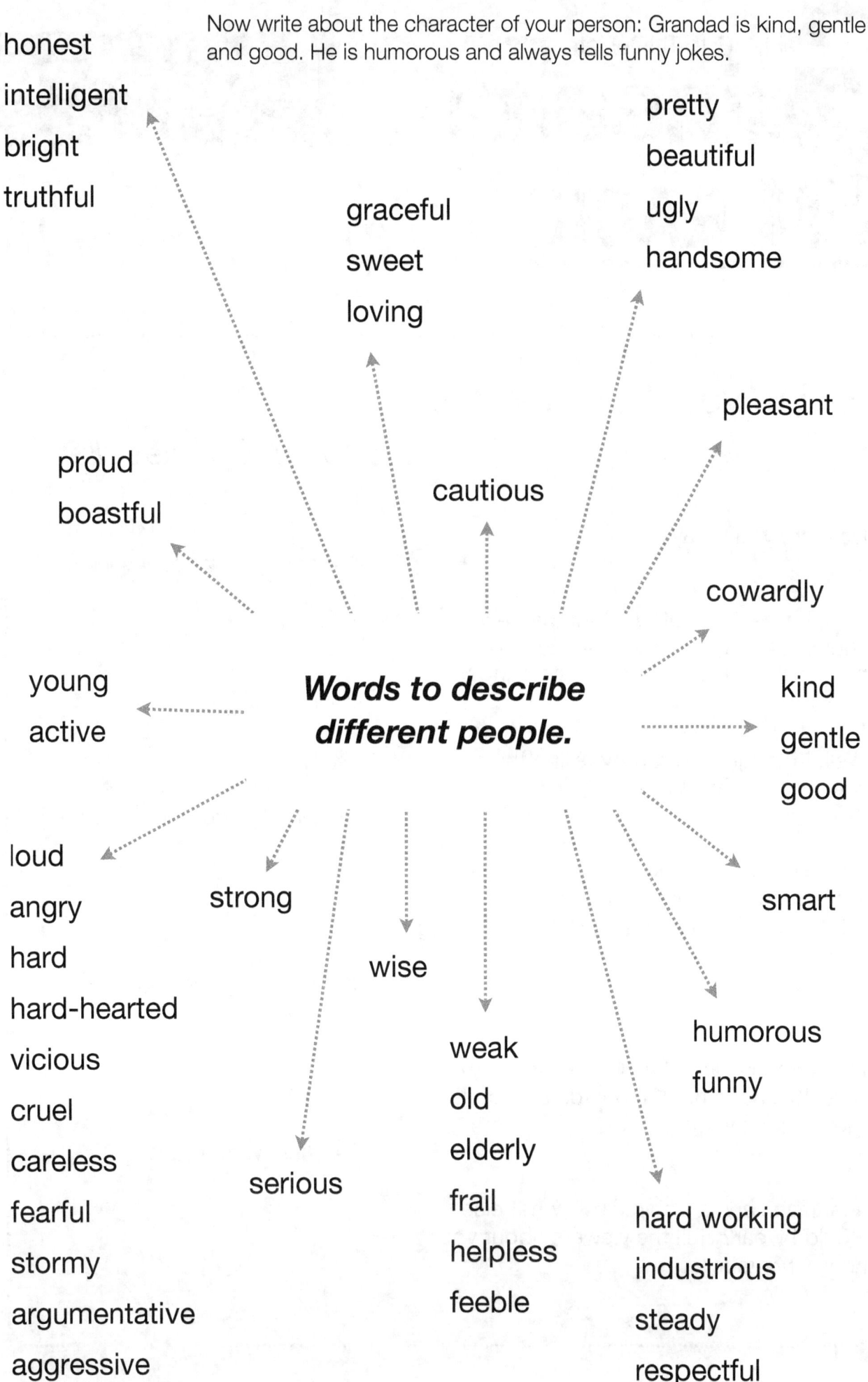

Listen Live

Hi, I'm your D.J. George:

... and I'm Christabelle:

How are you today?

I'm good. How about you?

Well, I'm really excited about the new show. We've got two whole hours to play all the music of our favorite bands.

That will be great!

Well, I thought I'd start by telling the listeners a little bit about myself.

That'll be interesting.

I'm George. You probably haven't seen me – because I only do radio, so I thought I'd describe myself. I'm a tall guy, with long brown hair.

It is very long and tied back in a ponytail.

I've got sparkling, blue eyes and very big ears. I've got a bit of a beard. Do you think they'll imagine me?

Tell them what you wear.

Just jeans and a t-shirt. Well, what else would I wear? Tell the viewers about you now, Christabelle.

Listen Live

I've got long, blonde hair down to my waist. My eyes are green. I wear bright pink lipstick. I'm medium sort of height.

and tell them what you like to wear...

'Fashion'... I like to wear whatever is in fashion: pretty dresses, patterned shirts, loose smock tops and pants in bright colors.

Anyway, just log onto the Rushford FM website and you will be able to see us on the web cam.

I've been a D.J. for fifteen years. How about you Chrissy?

I finished college last year so this is my first job..

So there you are, listeners. What are we like?

We're generally nice guys aren't we?

Yes, we always try to be kind ... good... and patient. Well, most of the time!

"Today I want the listeners to tell us about the **people they know**. People lead different lives. There are people who are public figures, people who work in different places and people who stay at home. They can be young or old, athletic, disabled or artistic. They all look different, some tall or short and some wearing glasses. They come from different backgrounds - some are rich, some poor. They have different homes and interests and achievements.

Think about all the different types of people you know. What do they look like? How do they behave? It could be someone in your family, a neighbor, or a friend.

We'll give the person with the best description a couple of tickets to Glitzy Mitzy's sold out gig on Saturday. Get texting or emailing in," says George.

My Mom has bright, green eyes and brown hair. She wears black rimmed glasses, but she always balances them right on the end of her nose.

Sarah writes...

My Nan is big, round and jolly, but she always looks amazing. She is also kind and generous and works hard as an ambulance driver taking sick people to the hospital.

Grumpy old Bertie has a wrinkled up face and thinning grey hair. He peeps out from behind the curtain and tries to catch children stealing his beautiful roses. He clenches his teeth and bangs on the window.

"How awful!"

Ryan texts...

My friend Dan has curly, black hair and brown eyes. Although he is in a wheelchair, he is the most sporty person I know and has won lots of awards.

"Cool!"

"We have Sophia on the line.

Hello Sophia. What is your story?"

"My Aunt May has blonde curly hair and blue eyes. She laughs a lot and chats to everyone. She knows everyone on her street and helps the older people do their shopping, if the weather is bad."

"Wow! What a kind lady."

Miss Prim is slim now and always looks neat and tidy. She hates it if our street is messy, so she goes out and picks up all the pieces of litter.

My Dad has a large belly because he eats too many fries.

My Uncle Pete is big. He is getting bigger and bigger. He is so big he broke his toilet seat.

| New | Reply Reply all Foward | Delete Mark as ▼ Move to ▼ |

INBOX (240)

FOLDERS

Junk (109)

Drafts (11)

Sent

Deleted (15)

New Folder

People You Know

☐ D.J. George
To George@guineapig.co.uk

1/15/15
Reply

My dad is very sunburnt because he went to Spain for the weekend. His face is bright red and his skin is peeling. He forgot to take his sunscreen!

Nadine

"That's dangerous."

Ben emails...

After dinner, my Grandad reads his paper. He wrinkles his brow, then his lids get heavier and heavier until his eyes shut tight. Then his head flops down. When I shout "Boo" he jumps out of his skin.

"That's great - keep them coming."

Sabrina has texted...

Naughty Neil is a bad kid with an angry expression. He is extremely agile. If his ball comes over the fence, he bangs on the door and if my Dad says he can't get it, he climbs over and gets it himself.

Phillip emails...

My teacher always looks fed up. Worse than this, she has a long bony finger which she points at the noisy children in my class.

Hannah texts...

Mr. Smith works in the city. He wears a suit to go to work and carries an umbrella. On Sunday, he washes his sports car until it shines and he can see his face in it.

Grandad smiles more than anyone else I know. He tells jokes all the time, but if I ask him to help me with my homework he always knows the right answer.

Michael texts...

Francie is so sweet and cute. She has round cheeks, blue eyes and no hair. She is always happy and she chuckles as she bangs her toys together. She is only six months old, but her Mom would love some tickets.

Christian is cool because he has very long, brown hair that reaches his waist. He plays in a rock band, so he practices his drums all the time. We can't hear ourselves think.

I am:

How many verbs or doing words can you spot? 'I am combing.'

- combing my long blonde hair.

- brushing out my short, frizzy curls.

- bouncing on my trampoline... or is it the sofa.

- shading my eyes from the bright sun.

- frowning because the cat is sleeping on my clean blanket.

- looking into my cat's green eyes.

- stroking my pony's long mane.

- caressing my dog's silky hair.

- staring up into my favorite pop star's eyes... but only on a poster.

- scoring my third goal of the game, thinking I am a super star.

- riding my mountain bike daringly, falling 'splat' into the mud.

- eating some cupcakes from the tin (but Mom doesn't know).

- wearing bright purple shorts.

- skipping to keep fit.

- seeing Mom wear her best outfit at the school gate, which means we're going somewhere.

- playing a dance game on my Wii, scoring thousands of points.

- doing a cartwheel on the grass to show off to my friends.

Now write some more sentences starting with 'I Am...'.

Write a detailed description about someone you know. Do not write his or her name.

Remember

1. **Introduction**
   Details of appearance (color of hair, eyes, height, size).

2. **Interesting points** about the **person's character** (always happy, kind).

3. **Interesting points** about the **person's activities** and **habits** (what he does, where he works, his or her hobbies, favorite food, sports).

4. **How do you feel** about that person.

5. Write a **suitable ending**.

   Now get someone to guess who you have written about.

Now that you know how to make interesting characters, you can use them in your stories.

When you write about people, you need to know: what they look like, what kind of people they are, the way they speak and behave, the way they feel, what they do.

The new principal and her husband want to buy a house, close to the school. Mr. Bruce Dangerfield, the real estate agent, asks them:

What is your <u>ideal</u> house?

My ideal house:

townhouse
semi-detached house
detached
bungalow
apartment
trailer
house boat
stables
shed
an old property with original features
Victorian

It has:

a new kitchen   marble countertops   wooden cabinets

new paint   a long narrow hall   a fireplace   a cellar

a play room   an en suite bathroom   central heating

a utility room   a study   a greenhouse   an attic   a cat flap

a big garden   a small garden   a swimming pool   a flower garden

Now let's brainstorm streets:

Do they want a house...

What is your <u>ideal</u> location?

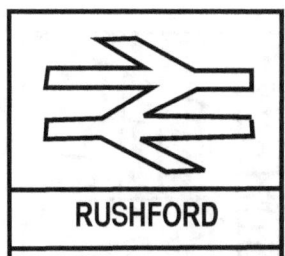

- in the town
- in the country
- in the city
- near the airport
- near the highway
- on a main road
- on a quiet road
- near the river
- near the stores
- near the train station
- near the local school
- near the park

Should the house...

- be on a street
- be on an avenue
- be on an estate
- be a new build
- an old period property

Fill in the missing words:

My ideal house is a ………………………………………… It has ……………
………………………………………………………………………………………………
………………………………………… The house will be ……………………………
………………………………………………………………………… which is …………
………………………………………………………………………………………………

FOR SALE
44 Acacia Road, Rushford

Photos: Outside View - Kitchen - Master Bedroom

Features:

- Built 1984
- Detached
- Carpeted Living Room
- New Kitchen
- Dining Room
- Study
- Coat Room
- 4 Bedrooms
- 2 Bathrooms and en suite.
- Double glazing
- Central Heating
- Spacious front and back yards.

This large detached house has been well looked after and it has a lovely garden full of flowers.

The large living room has a white marble fireplace and an efficient gas fire that will keep you warm on winter days. There are four wall lights. The patio door leads into the garden.

The spacious kitchen has an oven, dishwasher, a fridge and a freezer as well as a row of wood cabinets. There is a separate utility room where you can put the washing machine. The dining room leads to the kitchen.

There are nine rooms in total, including four big bedrooms, a downstairs coatroom and a bathroom with sink and toilet. The master bathroom has blue and white patterned tiles. The largest bedroom has large closets and an en suite with a power shower.

Mrs. Barker says to her class, "How would you describe your house, if you were a real estate agent who is selling it?"

Sam writes...

It is a large semi-detached house in a quiet street near the town center and train station. There are six rooms including a living room, a dining room and a big, cozy kitchen. All of the bedrooms have closets and there is a bathroom with blue tiles. There is a pretty yard full of flowers.

 Now it is your turn to write. How would you describe your house if you were a real estate agent?

You show someone around your house. Would they buy it? What do they like? What do they not like?

Make two groups. Add to the list 'I like it because...', 'I don't like it because...'

I LIKE IT BECAUSE...	I DON'T LIKE IT BECAUSE...
It is cozy.	The floorboards are creaky.
It is near the school.	There is a factory nearby.
....	....

The hall is too long and narrow.

It has a steep flight of steps.

It has three floors.

It has a dark cellar with steep steps.

It is two hundred years old.

The floor boards are creaky.

It is musty, dark, dingy and damp.

It is light and airy.

The kitchen needs modernizing.

It is too small.

It has bright wall lights.

The rooms are big.

In one of the bedrooms, there is no room for a bed.

The paint is peeling off the walls.

There is water leaking through the roof.

It is untidy and cluttered.

It has a large garden with lots of flowers.

The furniture is old and worn.

It is near the stores and school.

It has soft carpet.

There is a factory nearby with a smoky chimney.

There is only one bathroom.

The train tracks are close to the house.

It is clean and tidy.

There is a large marble fireplace in the living room.

It has a stylish and elegant interior.

It has a spacious, open-plan kitchen.

There is a patio door leading to a pretty garden.

The house has recently been decorated.

The bathroom has patterned tiles.

It is cozy.

It has lovely wallpaper.

It has room to build a swimming pool.

It is near the park and gym.

It is near a recycling center.

The bedrooms all have closets.

Mrs. Barker asks her class to write about a room in their house.

I love to sleep in on my soft bed with its yellow cotton quilt. I read my favorite book there. On summer days, I feel the warm sun burning down on me through the window.

I like to use my computer in my own room, where everything is mine. I look at all my computer games in colorful cases and the books arranged on my shelf. The brown teddy I brought back from Spain looks down on me from the shelf. My C.D. player is positioned on my desk next to my pot of pens.

I like to climb into the attic when I'm on my own. It is my own space, where no one comes. I sort through crates of stored stuff – clothes, old tapes and books. Up there, I smell a strange odor of musty old things. I can hang around up in the attic and no one cares.

I love the garage because it is stacked with fascinating gadgets and shiny tools. I sit on crates stored there and chat with Dad, as he bangs nails in with the hammer.

I love to snuggle down (in the lounge on my favorite armchair) next to my cat and watch my favorite T.V. programs, on the satellite channel on our new wide screen T.V.

Our kitchen is my favorite room. It is big, spacious and painted deep orange. It always smells of baking cakes and steaming casseroles – which makes me feel hungry. I like to watch my cats slurping their water and gobbling down their food. Mom chats to me as she stirs a pan of spicy curried chicken on the burner and lets me taste the spicy contents left on the spoon.

I like to soak in a steamy bath in the bathroom for twenty minutes and smell the sweet perfume of the bubbles. I also like to sail the soap like a boat, until Mom calls me to get out.

Now it's your turn. List the rooms you have in your house. Which is your favorite one? Write why you like this room.

My Bedroom

Plan:

What should I include?

Decide which paragraph (1, 2 or 3) each subject should go into. You should start a new paragraph if there is a change of time, or place, or event in your writing

- in the morning
- at night
- special toys
- furniture
- untidy
- my sister
- my cat
- my books/desk
- my bed/blanket
- how I feel

My bedroom is quite large and it has a soft woollen carpet, which feels warm on your toes. The walls are painted pale cream to match the lined curtains. A huge wooden bunk bed stands on the right side of the room which I share with my sister. On the top bunk, my cat stretches out, though he knows he's not allowed to be there. The white bookshelves are cluttered and some of the books have tumbled over. There is a collection of porcelain dolls that smile down at me.

I enjoy being alone in my bedroom – all by myself. I can hide away in my own little space with my cat. If I have a lot of homework, I sit at my desk reasoning out math questions or working on my project. When I have finished, I relax by sprawling myself across the floor to play a game or watch T.V. When my naughty little sister comes in, I get annoyed because she takes off her uniform and tosses it on the floor. She gets everything out of her closet because she is searching for some casual clothes to put on. I start yelling, "Clean up the mess!" My cat leaves the room sulkily and Mom comes up the stairs angrily to tell us off.

At night, when my light goes off, my room changes into a dark and secret place. The moon shines brightly through the gaps in the curtains, forming grey patterns on the carpet that are like bats skimming through the trees. An owl hoots outside, but my sister snores softly below. Then I snuggle down under my patterned blanket and read my exciting story book, where I get transported into a world of make believe. Finally, I start to doze off.

Now it is your turn to write. Answer the questions below to help you.

My House

- Where do you live?

- What is the name of your town?

- What is the name of your street and the number of your house?

- What kind of house do you live in? (detached, semi-detached, townhouse, bungalow, or apartment)

- How many bedrooms do you have?

- What other rooms are there?

- Choose a room in your house. It might be your own bedroom. Write down as many interesting things about the room as you can.

    - the furniture in the room
    - the color of the paint or wallpaper
    - the feel of the carpet or curtains
    - the view from the window
    - what do you like about this room?
    - Is it a quiet or a noisy place?
    - Are there gadgets, electronic games, ornaments, collections of books, special toys?

The children in Mrs. Barker's class make a huge wall picture (mural) for the community center of their local neighborhood.

They get into groups to discuss what they will put in it. They draw a map.

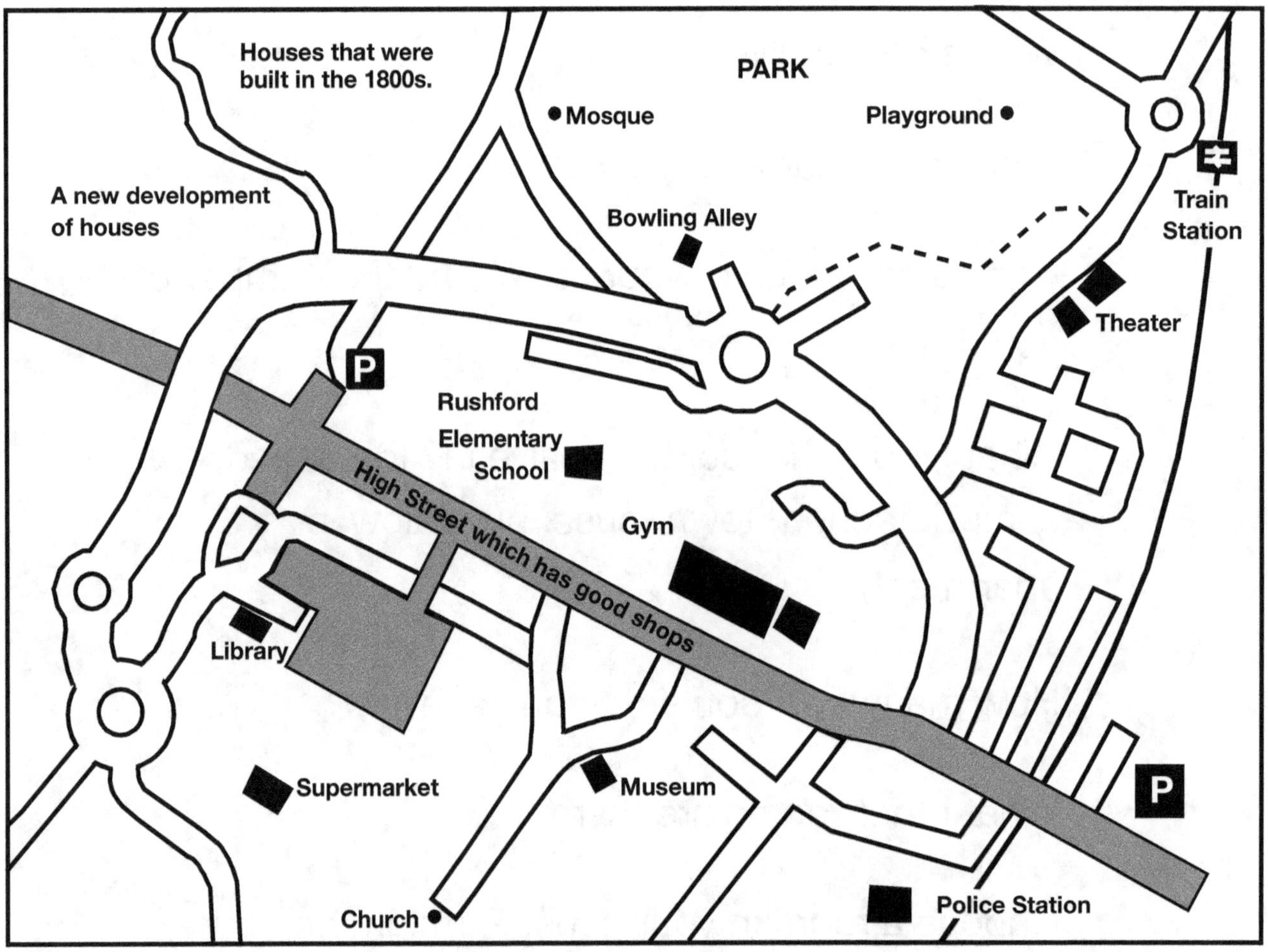

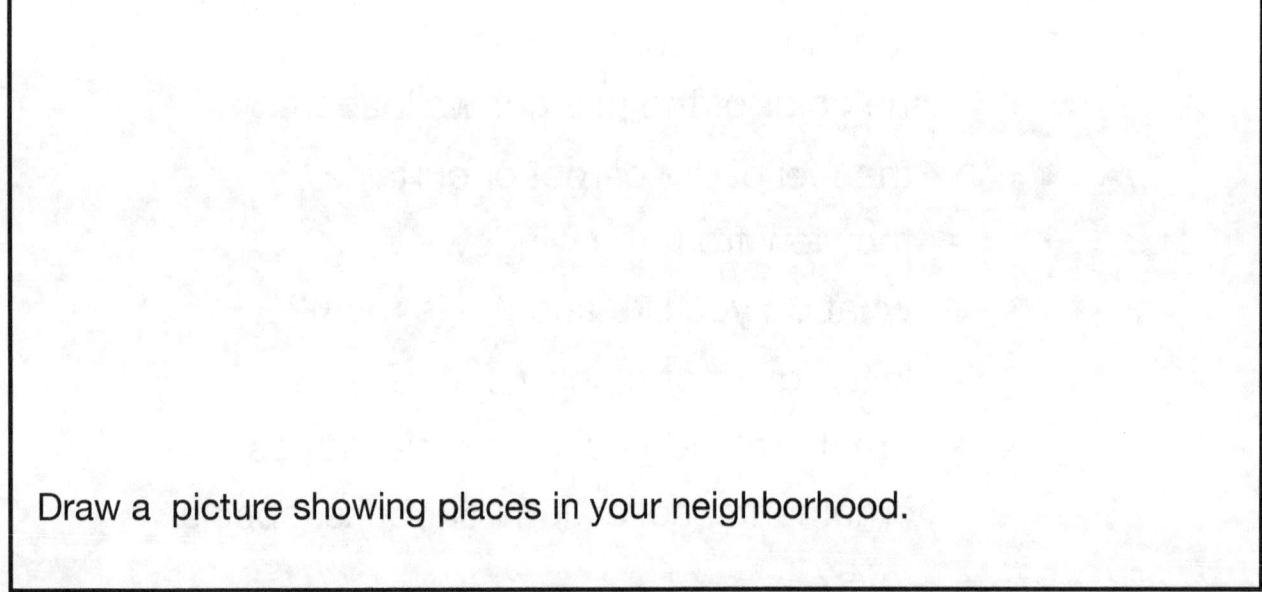

Draw a map of your town. Make a list of places in your area.

Draw a picture showing places in your neighborhood.

Mrs. Barker's class writes about their street on a summer's day..
Use the map to complete the sentences.

Our street is only a three minute walk from High Street so ……………………
………………………………………………………………………………………………………
………………………………………………………………………………………………………

On the corner, there is a garage that ……………………………………………………
………………………………………………………………………………………………………

By the supermarket there is a library, where you ……………………………………
………………………………………………………………………………………………………
………………………………………………………………………………………………………

The station is always busy because ………………………………………………………
………………………………………………………………………………………………………

There are several restaurants including …………………………………………………
………………………………………………………………………… so you can ………………
………………………………………………………………………………………………………

In the park you can ……………………………………………………………………………
………………………………………………………………………………………………………

Pretty flowers grow in the gardens of the ………………………………………………
………………………………………………………………………………………………………
………………………………………………………………………………………………………

At the sports stadium or gym you can……………………………………………………
………………………………………………………………………………………………………

Some people go to the church/mosque/temple to ……………………………………
………………………………………………………………………………………………………

Down our street, you see these people (people walking dogs/moms pushing their babies in strollers/Teenagers/Children helping people by cleaning cars/ Builders doing building work/ People selling door to door) ……………………………………………
………………………………………………………………………………………………………

You also see these animals, birds, insects ………………………………………………
………………………………………………………………………………………………………

Write some sentences about your own neighborhood.

What is the street like on a summer's night?

Isaac and Josh camp out in their tent.

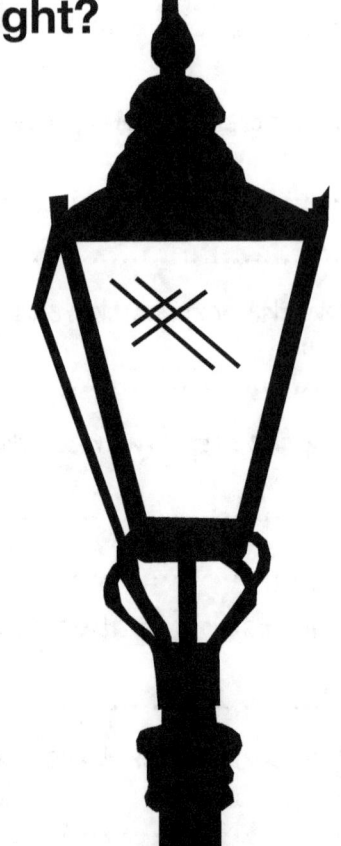

Isaac and I camped out at night.
We looked to the moon to give us light.

We tried so hard to get some sleep,
But out of the tent we had to peep.

The street lamps cast a golden glow
And shadows on the path did grow.

A black cat walked across the gate,
So we knew it was getting rather late.

The fox was going through the trash.
He knocked it over. What a crash!

An owl was hooting in the tree.
A scary noise for Isaac and me.

Hedgehogs searched the grass for scraps,
As a bat feasted on tasty gnats.

A buzzy thing flew through the air:
A stag beetle, a moth – it's nothing rare.

Lean Mrs. Twitch put out her cat,
Saw Mr. Fizz and stopped to chat.

Jon bedded down in a shop doorway,
While Alex parked in the residents' bay.

Dan and his dog took their nightly stroll
And sat on a bench to eat a cheese roll.

Back in the tent, it's time to sleep,
Forgetting the things in the night that creep.

CRASH, BANG, WALLOP!
"AH! AH! AH!
WHAT WAS THAT?"

Each verse has rhyming couplets.

Write the story about the day Isaac and his friend Josh camped out at night.

Sam says,

> "My address is 23 Fairtree Avenue, Rushford. There are different kinds of houses in our street, including detached houses, semi-detached houses, apartments and bungalows. There is a popular Indian restaurant at the end of our block where people eat in the evening. It serves delicious meals like Chicken Tikka Masala."

Kim says,

> "Our street is quite busy in the morning because people are leaving for work in their cars or walking to the station. Some car drivers use our road to get to High Street.
>
> The houses on our street have walls, fences and gates. They are neat and tidy. Most of the houses have pretty gardens with tubs of flowers and hanging baskets, except for one house, which is empty so the garden is overgrown. The pavement is quite wide and there are some tall trees, which look pretty in spring."

Sam says,

> "There is a playground in the park, only 5 minutes from my house. I play football with my friends there and we have fun on the play equipment."

Now you are learning to describe places using little details.

You can use details to create settings in the stories you write. If you describe the setting well, you will make your reader picture the place in his or her mind.

Write about your street.

Dan, the milkman, smiles whatever time it is in the morning.

Mr. and Mrs. Bold are quite old, but they are so kind, friendly and helpful.

Violet Moore knocks on the door to sell perfumes, powders and lotions.

Mr. and Mrs. Wong work all day long, but stop to chat on weekends.

Mr. and Mrs. Glen have a fine garden because they weed, prune and water plants all day.

Our window cleaner, Pete McThistle, scrubs the windows as clean as a whistle.

Zog, the dog, goes for a jog with his owner every day.

Baby B is as cute as can be because she gurgles, coos and grins in her stroller.

The people down our street are... quite nice.

Choose some of these characters. Plan and write a story about them.

Mrs. Twitch is as weird as a witch because she wears a black cloak, leans on a broom and talks to her black cat.

Mr. Sawyer is a lawyer and he is quiet, thoughtful and very smart.

Mrs. Bernard works hard as she brushes, sweeps and tidies all day long.

Mr. Fizzy makes me dizzy. He moves so fast as he goes past.

The evil cats are as bad as rats. They hiss and bite and scratch and fight.

Find some similes (weird as...)

Find some adjectives (cute, quiet, smart).

Sid, the bad kid, bangs on our door, is rude to my Dad and climbs the wall to get his ball.

Find some verbs or action words (she sweeps, gurgles, grins).

Now it is your turn to write about your street and your neighbors.

Answer these questions in sentences:

- Where is your street?

- What is the name of your street?

- What sort of houses are there on your street?

    (detached, semi-detached, apartments, bungalows or townhouses?)

- Are there other buildings? (offices, restaurants, shops.)

- Is your road quiet or noisy?

- Is it a busy main road near the town?

- Is there a lot of traffic on your road? What sort of traffic drives down your road? (buses, cars, vans)

- Where does your road lead?

- Draw a map of your road and the roads or footpaths that lead from it.

- What is your road like?

- Are the houses neat and tidy?

- Do they have gardens? Are they pretty?

- Are there driveways, trees and shrubs?

- Are the houses old or new?

- Do the houses have fences, paths or lawns?

- Are you allowed to play outside?

- What games do you play?

- Can you think of anything interesting that has happened on your street?

- Who lives on your street?

- Is it a friendly place?

- Are there some interesting neighbors on your street?

- Why are they interesting? Write down some interesting facts about them.

- What jobs do they do?

- What have they said or done?

- Name some more people you know there.

- Are the people on your street old or young?

- Who are your friends on the street?

- Do children play together? Do adults chat?

- Name the children who play together.

- Choose one of your friends who lives on your street, a child or an adult. Write a description - their appearance, character and interests. Now ask someone to guess who you have written about.

- What pets live on your street?

- What are they like?

- Is there any other wildlife living on your street?

Sam writes about his School

When I go to school, I travel with my mom in the car. I leave my house at 8:30 am and it takes us 20 minutes to get to school. If it is a sunny day, I walk to school with my friend Frank. If it rains ....

What else could Sam say?

I go to Rushford School, which is in Rushford. My teacher's name is Mrs. Smith and she is quite strict. She is tall, with dark, curly hair ....

....

What else could Sam say about his teacher?

Our classroom is big and it has an interactive white board. The teacher displays our best work on the wall ....
....

What else do you think Sam has in his classroom?

My favorite subject is definitely P.E. because I am crazy about football. I like English if I can write a story, but I find math difficult because I have to learn my tables. It is easy to add, take away and multiply, but when I have to divide - or do fractions, decimals or percentages - I find these very hard. My teacher gives us lots of homework and I have to learn my spelling and read my reading book ....
....

What other work could Sam write about?

I don't like my school uniform because I have to wear slacks and I prefer to wear jeans. I don't like the color of my sweatshirt because it is grey.

Draw Sam in his school uniform and label your drawing.

Some school lunches are delicious, but others are disgusting. Sometimes, I take a packed lunch which has some chips, a cheese sandwich, a chocolate cookie and an apple.

<u>Make a menu for school lunches</u> or design your perfect packed lunch. What food do you like? Why? What other lunches could you put on the menu?

MONDAY	**TUESDAY**	**WEDNESDAY**	**THURSDAY**	**FRIDAY**
Spaghetti and Meatballs	Roast Beef Sandwiches	Chicken Curry	Cheese Pizza	Burgers and Fries
Chocolate Pudding	Ice cream	Rice Pudding	Coconut Custard	Yogurt and Fruit

I like school because I see my friends Frank and Peter. We play football on the school team.

I like to sit next to Frank and Peter at the boys' table. Sometimes the teacher blames me for talking too much, then, I have to sit with the girls. I hate doing this.

I don't like this boy named Nigel, because he is always getting me into trouble.

Make a list of Sam's friends. Write down some more things they do in school. Remember Sam's sister Kim? Write a list of Kim's friends. Write down some things she enjoys doing at school.

Parent-Teacher Conferences

Sam's parents go to a parent-teacher conference and they look through pile of Sam's work that he left on his table.

Mom: How's he doing?

Dad: *(holding Sam's book up)*
This writing is a bit scruffy and he has only written ten lines on this page.

Mrs. B: Well, he's concentrating a bit better, but sometimes his writing is messy and it takes him a long time to get his English tasks done.

Dad: Does he know his multiplication tables?

Mrs. B: No, he needs to practice them everyday.

Mom: What can we do to help?

Mrs. B: Make sure he practices his reading book every day and learns his spelling. He could keep a diary too. It will help him to improve his writing. Practice the hard tables too - 6 x 7, 7 x 6.

Mom: Is he paying attention in class?

Mrs. B: He talks a lot. He is better if he sits at the girls' table ....
....

.... : ....
....
....

.... : ....
....
....

Continue the dialogue.

Write some dialogue between your teacher and your parents at a parent-teacher conference.

End of Spring Report Card: Samuel Carter

Math	Sam tries hard but he needs to learn his tables.
English	Sam needs to practice reading longer words. He needs to use punctuation in his writing.
History/Geography	Sam's handwriting needs to be improved.
French	Sam needs to participate more in class.
Science	Sam must try to listen more, especially when we are doing experiments.
Art	Sam has an artistic flair, but he is much too messy. He spilled a can of paint last week all over the floor
P.E.	Excellent. Sam enjoys P.E. and it shows. He is on the school football team.

End of Spring Report Card: Frank Simpson

Math	Excellent progress. Frank is working on the highest level.
English	Frank's writing is very interesting. He uses lots of verbs, adjectives and adverbs in his excellent stories.
History/Geography	Very neat project work.
French	Speaks French very well.
Science	Frank always takes a great interest in science. He puts his hand up in class to ask questions.
Art	Frank is very talented.
P.E.	Average

What are Sam's favorite subjects? What subjects does Frank enjoy most?

Now it's your turn: Write an imaginary report for you or a friend.

There are eight classes in Sam's school. They take turns leading the assembly. Mrs. Barker says, "It is our turn to do the assembly. It will be about recycling."

She says that the class must find out about recycling for homework. The children do some research at home and they find out information. They use books, they talk to a man at the city council office and they use the web.

What does Sam find out? What does he draw?

Recycling

- Recycle 32% of our garbarge

- You can recycle clothes, C.D.'s plastic, batteries, glass, paper.

- It is very important to recycle because landfill sites very full.

- ....

The Recycling Logo

What is recycling?

It is converting waste into reusable material.

The teacher helps her class put the ideas together. They write a script for assembly and draw some pictures to hold up.

Friday July 7th, Rushford School - Green Class assembly.

Frank: Welcome to our assembly on recycling. Did you know the United States produces over 250 million tons of garbage every year, but we only recycle 32% of it? Some garbage, that could be recycled, ends up in the landfill site and that's really harmful for the environment we live in.

Kelly: **We're going to tell you how recycling saves you energy.**

Neesha: One recycled tin can save enough energy to power a T.V. for three hours.

Nina: One recycled glass bottle can save enough energy to power a computer for 25 minutes.

Ryan: One recycled plastic bottle can save enough energy to power an 80 watt light bulb for 3 hours.
(The children hold up paintings they've done.)

Aaron: If you recycle all paper, it will stop 24 trees from being chopped down.

Sam: Families throw away, in their garbage, almost 100 pounds of plastic bottles every year which could be recycled and they take 500 years to decompose (break down) if they are buried in a landfill site.

Laura: **We found out some facts about why you should recycle different materials.**

Josh: If we recycle all our cans made from aluminum, we would need 14 million fewer garbage cans.

Nigel: 60% of trash that ends up in our garbage can be recycled and will produce enough energy to power a T.V. for 5000 hours.

Isaac: All the trash that we throw away every day could fill some of the largest lakes in the world in just a few months.

Kegi: Every family uses about 500 glass bottles a year, but if you throw them away they will end up in a landfill site and never decompose. In 1000 years they'll still be there.

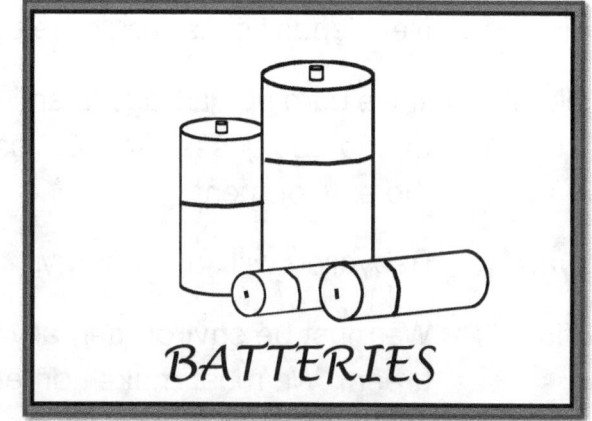

BATTERIES

(Mrs. Barker shows pictures using her computer.)

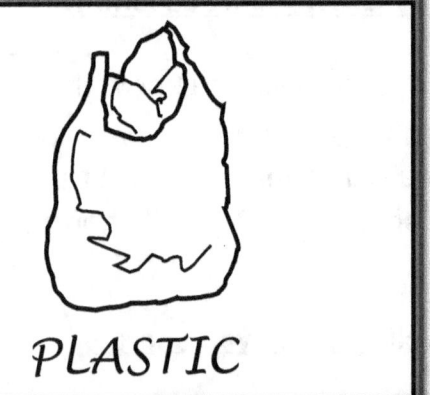
PLASTIC

GLASS

Candice:	Throwing away trash means throwing away materials that could be valuable.
James:	**Here are some materials you can recycle:** (The children show some evidence from things they've collected.)
Justine:	batteries
Ellie:	clothes
Jo:	C.D.s
Sara:	Aluminum cans.
Cassey:	Food and garden waste.
Jessica:	Paper and cardboard.
Portia:	Plastic.
Simon:	Glass.
Olivia:	**We found out some reasons why we must recycle.**
Noah:	Landfill sites are filling up. (The class show a big picture they've made together.)
Cole:	New landfill sites would be ugly and smelly.
Callum:	If we burn up garbage in an incinerator (fire) it will produce dangerous gases like CO2 carbon dioxide, which will be bad for the environment.
Priya:	Recycling will save energy.
Sofia:	We must be environmentally friendly. It feels good. We must go green. We must make something useful from materials that we no longer require.

Thank you for listening to our class assembly. We hope you have learned about recycling.

You can help this planet if you recycle. Take bottles to the recycling center and clothes to charity drives.

It is important to sort your trash into old food waste, cardboard and plastic.

You can put glass, cardboard and plastics in separate bins and the city will collect it at the recycling center.

"We live on a wonderful planet. Please help us look after it, so that people who live in the future will have a nice place to live."

Our teacher says, " ....
...."
Mrs. Jackson the principal says, " ....
...."
Parents say, " ...."

Plan out another topic for a school assembly. Draw out some cards.

If you are writing <u>fiction,</u> you are writing a story to entertain your reader, but if you write <u>non-fiction</u> you will write a leaflet, a report, a letter, diary or interview. You will inform your reader about something - explain something - advise - or instruct someone. You might even persuade someone to think like you.

Let's make a leaflet. You can use the facts that you learned about recycling. Write your facts under headings, so the reader can find the information quickly.

Start by introducing your subject.

Write:

1. It is very important to convert our garbage into reusable material or we will...

2. How recycling saves us energy.

3. Why we should recycle materials.

4. Materials we can recycle.

5. How we'll ruin our world if we don't recycle.

Conclusion

6. What I think about recycling?

1. Organize your non-fiction writing into paragraphs so you start a new one each time you write about a different subject. Each paragraph starts with a topic sentence or main idea. The rest of the paragraph will explain it.

2. You can link the paragraphs with the conjunctions below:

Also	Moreover	However	On the other hand
Despite this	Finally	Furthermore	Next
In contrast		In addition to	What is more

Sam talks about his Teacher.

What is her name?

My teacher's name is Mrs. Barker.

What does she look like?

She has dark brown, curly hair. Her eyes are blue and her cheeks are red. When she stands in front of the class, I see that she is quite tall and slim.

What does she wear?

On school days, she often wears black pants and a colorful sweater. Sometimes, she wears a long skirt, a flowery blouse and a pearl necklace that hangs around her neck.

What is her character like?

Mrs. Barker is always kind and her voice is gentle. She never shouts loudly. If you make a mistake, she says... "Well, that's a bit tricky isn't it? Let me show you."

What do you do with your teacher?

We do Math, English, French, History and Geography.

Write about your Teacher

My teacher is called ....
....

He/She has ....
....
....
....

On school days he/she wears ....
....
....
....
....
....

Mrs. .... or Mr. ....
is always ....
....
....
....

Make a list of the things you do with your teacher
....
....

What other teachers do you have? What do they teach you?

Mr. Green is mean. He teaches me to play the piano. He roars, "Play that again. It's all wrong. You haven't practiced. I'm having a word with your Mom."

I have ....
....
....
....
....

The funniest thing is...

Last winter Mrs. Barker lost her voice and she couldn't speak for three days. She had to write everything down or make signs with her hands.

My teacher..
....
....
....

The most serious thing is...

She sent naughty Nigel to the vice principal's office. He had to sit there through play time. Then he had to write a letter to apologize to Mrs. Barker for throwing things in class.

....
....
....
....
....

Name some teachers you had in other years. What were they like?

Miss Smith used to shout loudly all the time and go red in the face when she said... "Class 4, please be quiet....or ...Please keep the noise down...Please don't talk. DON'T TALK, I MEAN IT."

Describe them: ....
....
....
....
....
....

Now it's your turn to write.

Write about your School

- How do you travel to school? Is it by car, bus, train, bicycle or by foot?
- Is it a long journey? How long does it take you, from the time you leave your house until you reach school?
- Who drives you?
- What do you pass on the way to school?
- Do you get into a traffic jam?

- What school do you go to?
- What is your teacher like?
- What is your classroom like?
- Is there a display of work on the wall?
- What is your favorite subject?
- Why?

- How much homework do you have?
- Do you like school lunches or do you take a packed lunch?
- Do you like school? Why?

- Who are your best friends at school?
- Who do you play with at playtime?
- What do you play?
- What do you talk about?
- Does your class lead a school assembly? What subject did you do?

- What is your school uniform like?
- What color is it?
- What style is it?
- What shoes do you wear?
- Draw a picture of your uniform.

A TV program is looking for the world's BEST FRIEND.

Sam writes about his best friend:

"My best friend is a boy called Frank and he has blond hair and blue eyes. He is quite tall.

There are four people in his family, who are his mom, his dad and his sister Kelly. His mom works as a teacher in a school, but his dad works in the city. Since his parents work late, he comes over to my house every night.

Frank likes to wear jeans and a t-shirt, but he also loves his soccer uniform. Soccer is his favorite sport and he supports his favorite team, which is Rushford United.

On weekends, Frank and I play soccer, but we also play on our skateboards. If it rains, Frank helps me with my homework (he is smart) and we play a computer game.

I think Frank is a good friend because he is generous and kind."

Kim writes,

"My best friend is a girl called Candice, who has brown eyes and black curly hair, which she braids into tight braids with beads. She is quite tall and slim.

Candice has a mom and a big sister called Tamsin who is five years older than her. After school, she likes to go shopping and wears the latest fashionable clothes and shoes.

During the weekend, Candice goes to her performance academy (dancing class) to do ballet and tap. Then, she comes to my house for a sleep over and we stay up late to watch D.V.D.'s and play games like Monopoly.

I think Candice is always kind because she lends me her things."

Sam says,

"Write about your best friend. Write down everything you can remember, write… write…write…"

- Is your best friend a boy or a girl?
- How old is your friend?
- What is his/her name?
- How many are there in his/her family?
- Write down some details about his/her family.
- Where does he/she live?
- Write down some facts about his/her appearance.
- Is he/she tall, short, fat or slim?
- What is the color of his/her eyes, hair?
- What clothes does he/she like to wear?
- Now write about the things he/she likes to do.
- What are his/her favorite computer games or activities?
- What games do you like to play together?
- Lastly, what makes him/her a special friend?
- Is he/she kind, patient, helpful, generous?

Time to tune into Guinea Pig FM RADIO

Listen Live

It's time for the weekend. Let's turn on the radio to George's drive home show.

What are you going to do this weekend Christabelle?

I have to clean my apartment... and do the food shopping... and...

Come on! It's the weekend. You can't work all the time. Aren't you going to have some fun?

Well: I might go and see that new film. What is it called? Oh and I'm baby sitting my niece. I might go to the zoo and see the lions and tigers.

That's more like it.

How about you George? What will you be doing?

I'm heading off to the airport, to get a flight straight after the show. Guess where I'm going?

France, Holland, Spain...?

Nearly...

Cyprus?

You got it! I'm going to stay with a friend. We're going to spend the weekend by the pool and on the beach... relaxing.

Sounds great!

"Right, you listeners, we've just got time for you to send in what you'll be doing during the weekend," says George.

I will help my Grandad paint his fence, because he has arthritis in his arm and it hurts him to do it. Neil

Kayleigh emails…

My friend, Celine, is coming over for a sleep over. We are going to order a massive pepperoni pizza to eat between us. We'll play games, watch D.V.D's and talk, talk…until it is late and we fall asleep. I hope my teacher is not listening, because she'll know why I'm so tired on Monday.

I'm going to the sports center, with my friends, to have a great time splashing in the pool. We'll see who can go the fastest down the water slide. Then, we'll go to the movies and see the latest film. Afterwards we'll grab a burger and fries. It will be great fun.

Noah emails…

I'm going to play soccer in the park with my friend and see who can score the most goals - like I do every weekend. I'll watch my sister on the playground.

My mom and I will go shopping in the big stores in the city and buy fashionable clothes and shoes and jewelry.

Katherine

Harvey writes…

I'm going, with my Dad, to collect his new Audi. It is 'brand spanking new' and inside it will smell of leather. The blue paint work will be shiny. Dad will sit in the chair with the salesman and sign the papers. Then we will get in and Dad will start the engine and we'll drive out of the garage. It will be ours."

"Cool!"

Claire texts…

I'm taking my dog to classes to make him obey me... because he keeps racing off and running away. I have to chase him.

"We have Portia on the line.

Hello Portia. What is your story?"

"My friend Heather and I are going to a theme park and we are going on all the fast rides like – 'Terror Coaster' and 'Shock Extreme.' We're going to see who can scream the loudest as we whirl around and around."

"Wow! That's going to be fun."

I'm going to the big football game with my dad and uncle Fred. You'll be able to hear me cheering my team for miles if we win. Zack

I'm going to baby sit for my cousin's baby so she can go out to dinner. Lydia

Dad will take me fishing and we'll catch a huge carp. Cole

My friend and I will go to 'Feather World' bird park. I'll buy some bird seed which will be dried wiggly worms. I can't wait to see Tom's face when he has to feed them.

Rachel texts...

I'll go to the sea and have a picnic on the sand. I'll swim in the sea, but I'll probably come straight out because it will be freezing cold. The dog will also swim and shake his wet coat all over me.

Heather emails...

Mom, Louise, Simon and I will go to the out of town mall. We will get a burger for lunch and some fries. After Mom has finished her shopping, we will explore Pirate Pete's castle and his treasure ships. It is a mini-golf course so it will be fun to see if I can win. Next, Louise and I will go on the paddle boats on the lake for half an hour. We'll go to the end of the lake under the bridge. Then Simon will take a shot at climbing the rock face. Finally, we'll watch the swans and their three cygnets gobble up left over fries at the fast food restaurants. They'll want more!

I'll go to the big mall, but I'll go on the bouncing castle and then Mom will buy me an ice cream.

I'm going ice skating at the stadium on Sunday with my best friend. I'll slip and slide all over the place to begin with and have to cling to the sides so I don't fall over. It'll be fun. When we've finished, we'll have a cool glass of raspberry smoothie topped with whipped cream.

Write your own paragraph. Write about a dancing or drama class. Write about the sports you will do: wakeboarding, rafting, paintball or bowling or maybe you have been to a special occasion like a birthday party or a wedding.

What will **you** <u>do</u> if it *RAINS*?

Write down what you will do. Help the children to finish their paragraphs.

I'll play on my laptop computer. First, I'll download some information from the internet so I can finish my homework. Then ....
....
....
....
....
....
....
....
....

My friend Adam and I get all my Lego toys. They're in the garage in stacking boxes. We make a huge town from Lego blocks. It has ....
....
....
....
....
....
....
....
....

What can you do on a computer?

I can:
- surf the web
- speak to friends
- play games
- send emails
- print out information

Do you have a Lego set?

What can you make?

Draw your Lego Model

My Laptop Computer

Sam logs onto a website because he wants to find out some information for his science project. Draw and write what he sees, reads, and discovers. His project is about the water cycle. What should he enter into his computer? What comes up?

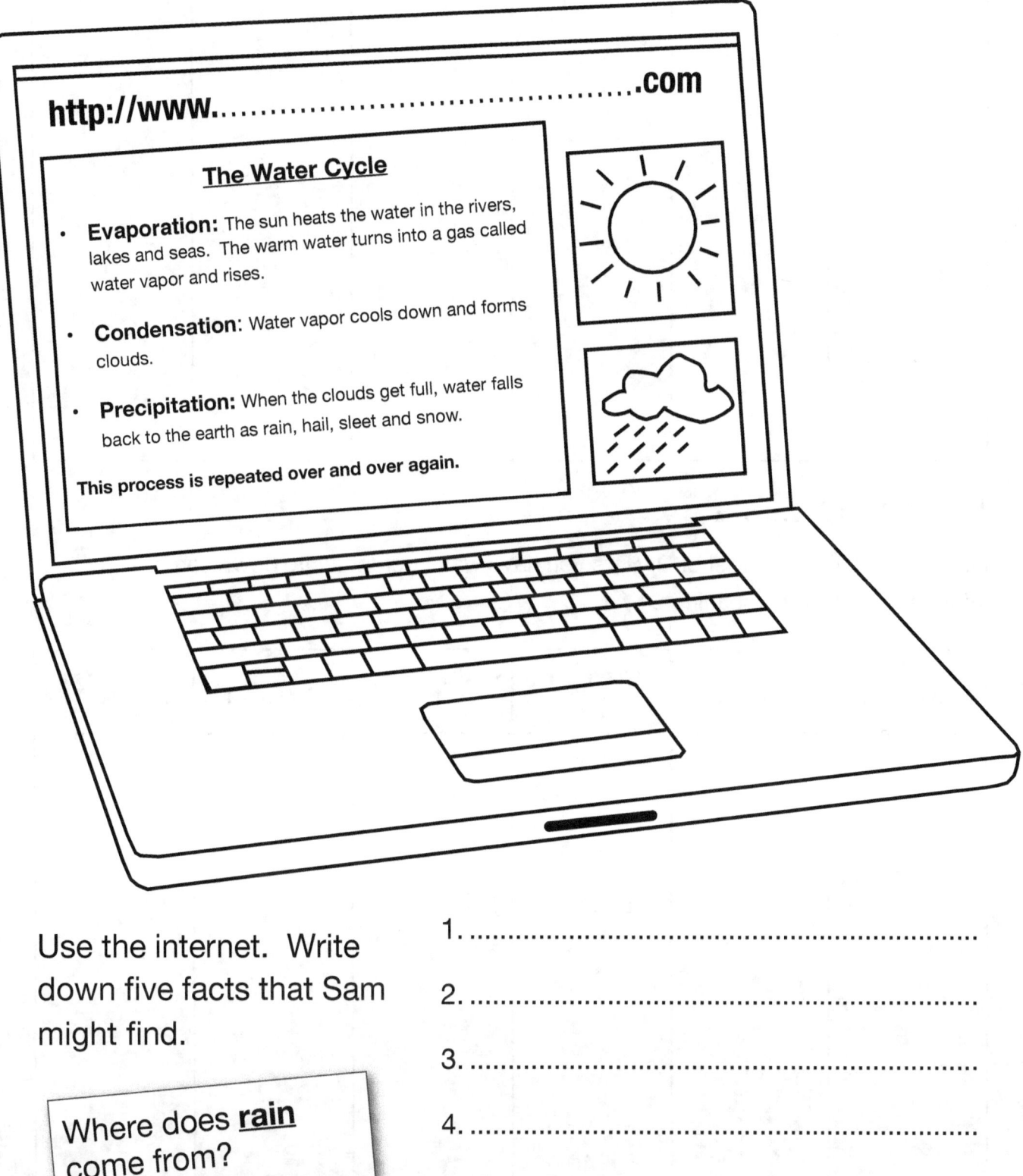

Use the internet. Write down five facts that Sam might find.

Where does **rain** come from?

1. ....
2. ....
3. ....
4. ....
5. ....

I watch T.V. on dull rainy days.

Fill in the chart. Make a list of programs that you watch and write down some information under the headings.

Time of Day	Program Channel	Characters	Setting	What is the Program about?	What I like about the program.

I watch D.V.D.'s

Fill in the chart. Make a list of D.V.D.'s you have watched and write down some information under the headings.

Name of D.V.D.	Who is in it?	Where is it set?	What is it about?	Why I like it.	What I do not like about it.

Answer these questions in a sentence. Use different words to start each sentence.

- What day is it on? Is it a series?
- What time is it on? Which channel?
- What is it called?
- What are the presenters called? Which characters appear in it?
- What happens in the program?
- Is it a cartoon, quiz, drama, soap, comedy or documentary?
- Write down some facts about this program.
- Is there a story to follow?
- Do the presenters show you how to make things?
- Do they tell you any facts - about nature, cars, other countries? If so, what facts do they tell you?
- Why do you particularly like this program?
- Do you have a favorite episode that you can remember? If so, why? Write about it.
- List any other programs that you watch on T.V.

My Cell Phone

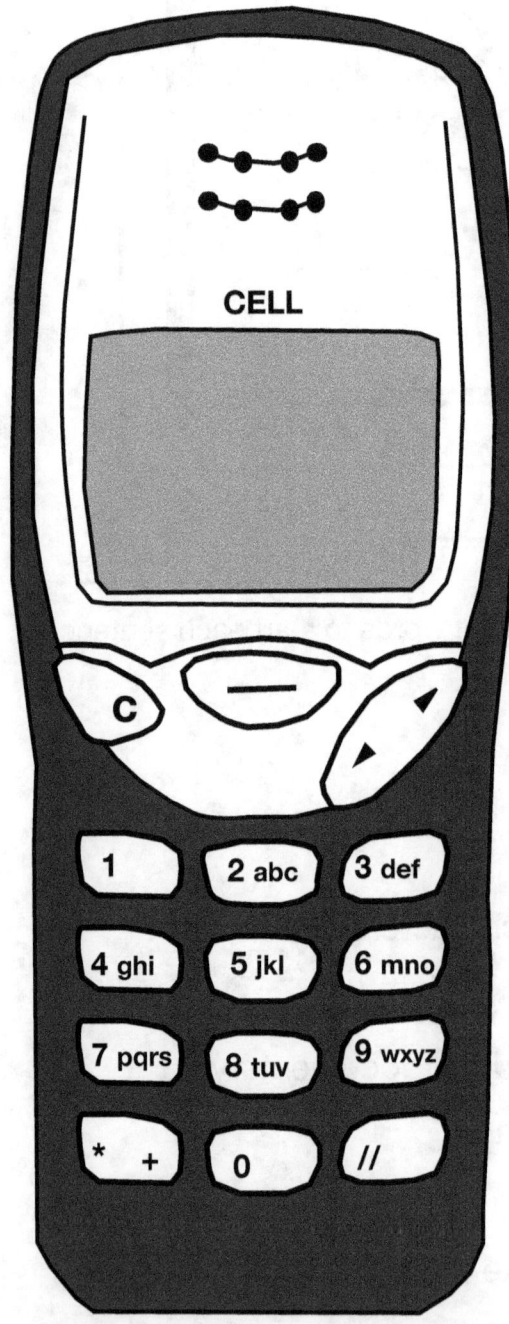

Answer these questions in a sentence.

- What kind of cell phone have you or your parents got?
- Does it have a touch screen or a keypad?
- Do you know the brand of your phone?
- Do you know who your service provider is?
- Who do you call?
- Why?
- What else can you do on your phone?
- Does your phone have a camera?
- What pictures do you take?
- Can you access and use the internet from your cell?
- Do you send text messages?
- Do you download music?
- Do you have an iPad?
- Do you have Skype?
- Who do you talk to?

Write a paragraph explaining how you use your cell phone.

Write:

It is useful to have a cell phone because...

Fill in these charts.

I listen to my favorite C.D.'s, which are...

Name of Band	Why I like them

Films I have seen at the movies and plays/musicals I have seen at the theater.

Name	Who is in it?	Where is it set?	What is it about?	Why I like it

Make a list of every computer game you own.

-
-

Explain how you play the games?
What do you have to do to win?
What is your highest score?

Make a list of your Nintendo Wii or PlayStation games.

-
-

Explain how you play the games?
What do you have to do to win?
What is your highest score?

Now, it is your turn to write about what interests you.

Write the answers to these questions in a sentence.

- What do you find interesting?

- What do you do when you get home from school?

- What do you do on weekends or the school holidays?

- What activities do you enjoy?

- Have you ever owned something that you think is really special? Tell us about it.

Do you own some special things you will keep forever, in a special place, drawer or box?

Write:

- When did you have them?
- Who gave them to you?
- Why are they special?

"The old train set is special because it was given to me by my great grandad when he was alive. It belonged to him when he was a boy so it is very old."

1. Make a list of your ten favorite toys or keepsakes.

2. Why did you like them?

Write:

My most treasured possession is ....
....
It is special because ....
....
It was given to me by my ....
....

My trampoline ...

My Ferrari remote control car ...

My brown bear ...

A soccer ball signed by ...

A china ornament from ...

My favorite book ...

My guitar ...

My PlayStation ...

Do you own something that is very special to you?

Read this page and then write about something you own.

Sam says,

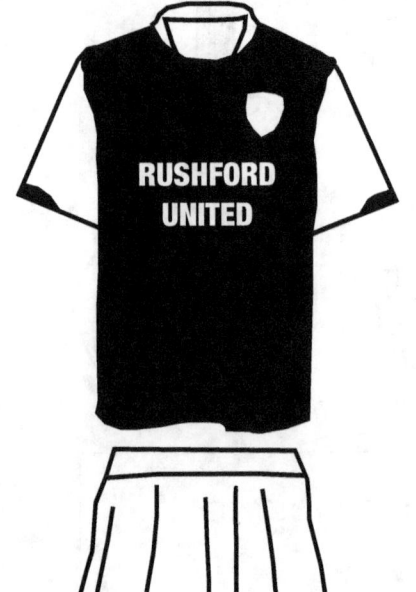

My remote control racing car sits on my shelf. It has super speed and independent suspension. Occasionally, dad and I take it on the pavement outside our house and we use the remote control to race it. I can't run it for long, because the batteries are expensive.

My most treasured possession is my soccer uniform, which supports my favorite team.

Kim says,

I have a cute teddy bear, called Sue, that my Nan gave me for my first Birthday. It has been cuddled so much, that its fur is all ruffled up.

When I was younger, I was given a life-sized toddler doll with batteries that talked to me. She had glitter print on her top. She could tell me when she needed her magic potty and you could hear it make flushing sounds. I could change her diaper. It was like a real baby.

Write about *your* most <u>memorable</u> BIRTHDAY.

I was .... years old.

Write about your favorite birthday card.

………………………………………
………………………………………
………………………………………
………………………………………
………………………………………
………………………………………

Write about the friends and relatives who came to your party.

………………………………………
………………………………………
………………………………………
………………………………………
………………………………………
………………………………………

Write about the presents that you received for your birthday.

………………………………………
………………………………………
………………………………………
………………………………………
………………………………………
………………………………………
………………………………………
………………………………………
………………………………………
………………………………………
………………………………………

Write about how you celebrated your birthday.

………………………………………
………………………………………
………………………………………
………………………………………
………………………………………
………………………………………

Ask Mom and Dad.

> **Do you have any special things that you keep?**
> **Where did they come from?**
> **Why are they special?**

"An old stamp collection, which belonged to my grandfather; it contains stamps from all over the world and some are extremely rare."

"A china jug, at least three hundred years old, that I bought from a junk shop. It is hand painted, in a pretty, blue pattern. I'm told it's worth hundreds of dollars."

"A teddy bear that I had as a child. It is very old and it is thread bare where I have cuddled it so much."

"An old painting – painted over two hundred years ago - and worth a lot of money."

"My photo album full of photos containing memories of all those special times over the years."

"A spear from Africa. It is carved with an intricate design. It is very unusual - a real collectors piece."

> Ask Frank:
> ## What does he own that is special?

I have all the Lego models so I can build whole towns. Sometimes I build a town with hospitals, airport and a harbor.

My little sister collects teddy bears, not real ones, but ones made of fabric. She has a complete set.

My most treasured possession is my soccer ball signed by a player from the team that I support, which I won in a competition. My best friend, Sam, is jealous because he would like one.

A day off school ...

pale face
ear ache
head hurts
eyes sting
runny nose
temperature up
body aches
sore throat
stomach ache
shivering
sick
cough
dizzy
upset stomach
faint
long faced
fever
awful
fed up
sad
terrible
dreadful
unhappy

dejected   depressed   painful

melancholy   down cast   gloomy   distressed

sorrowful   ghastly   miserable   appalling   tearful

> Have you ever woken up feeling awful? You can hardly lift your head off the pillow because it is throbbing. Your body aches all over, your throat is sore, your nose is running and you shiver and shake?

Sam woke up one morning just like this. He called to his mom, "I feel bad this morning. My head aches; when I sit up I'm all shivery."

"Let's take your temperature," replied Mom. "It's quite high," she continued, shaking the thermometer. "You must stay in bed. I'll call the doctor and get an appointment."

Later, Sam was sitting with Mom in Dr. Patel's waiting room. He had been there for more than half an hour which made him feel worse. He was dozing on the chair when the buzzer sounded and his name came up on the screen. It startled him so much that it made him jump. That made his head ache even worse.

The doctor sat by his computer, surrounded by bottles, flasks and piles of papers, "You have the flu," explained the doctor jovially. "There's a lot of it going around." He quickly typed a prescription. "Take three tablets a day. Stay indoors for a few days and you'll soon feel better," he beamed. As Sam left the office, he was feeling surprisingly much better. His symptoms were disappearing because he was making plans. He was deciding how he would use the time off school.

Shall I play with my PlayStation, or my Lego blocks? Shall I watch T.V. or a DVD? Shall I draw a picture? he thought.

Write three paragraphs saying how you woke up one morning with a bad cold or flu.

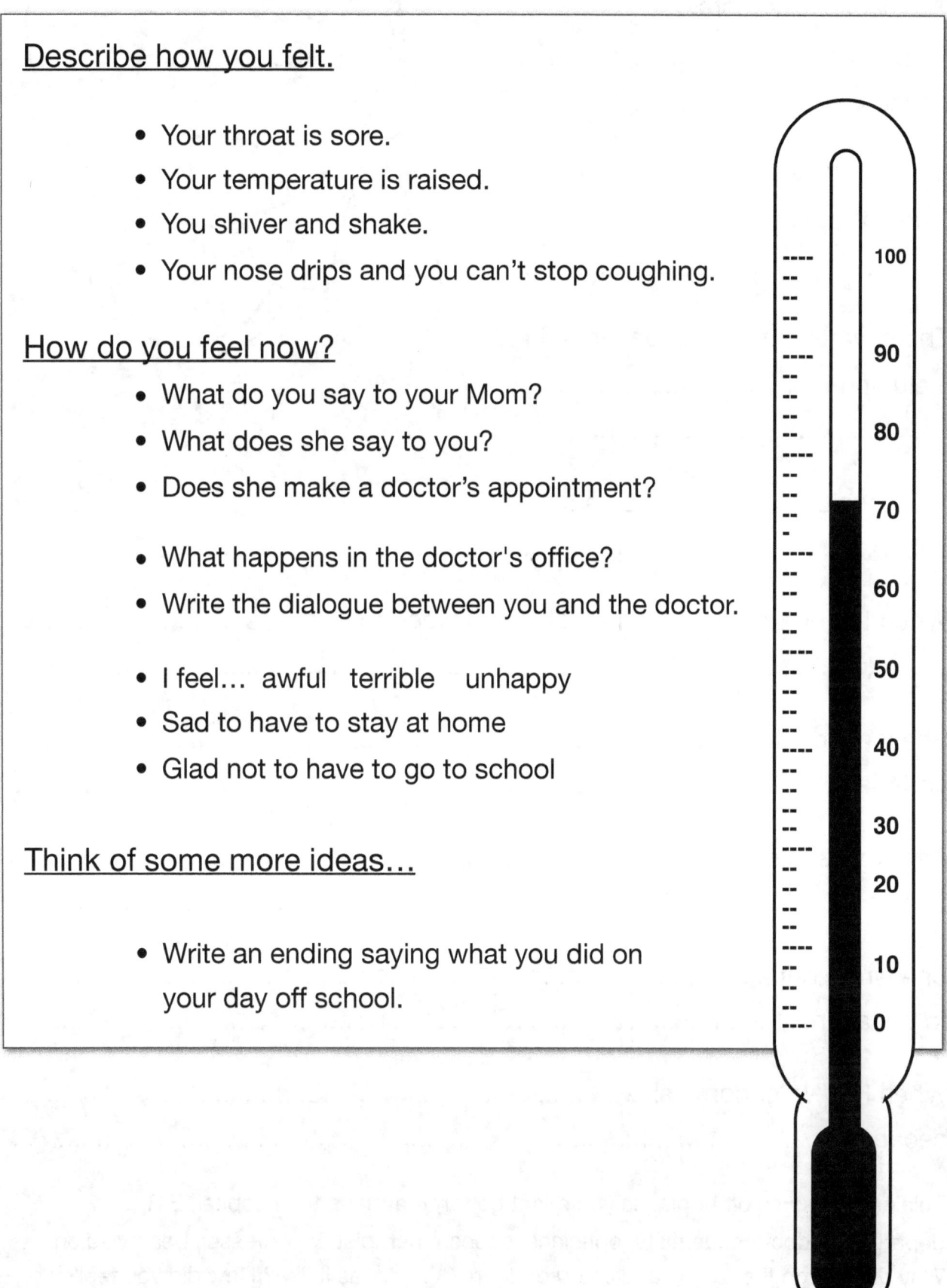

Describe how you felt.

- Your throat is sore.
- Your temperature is raised.
- You shiver and shake.
- Your nose drips and you can't stop coughing.

How do you feel now?

- What do you say to your Mom?
- What does she say to you?
- Does she make a doctor's appointment?

- What happens in the doctor's office?
- Write the dialogue between you and the doctor.

- I feel… awful   terrible   unhappy
- Sad to have to stay at home
- Glad not to have to go to school

Think of some more ideas…

- Write an ending saying what you did on your day off school.

Kim came home from school feeling awful, because......................................
....

She said to her mom,
"I can't go to...
because.."

Mom took her to the walk in clinic where they waited.............................
....

There were some other patients there including..................................
....

In the waiting room she also saw........
....

When the nurse saw her she took her temperature. It was.............................
....

She looked into her ....
and then..

After this she said, "......... ....
....

She wrote out a ....for.......................................
to be taken..

When Kim went home she ....
because..

Think about some other places you might go for treatment: the hospital, E.R. department, doctors, dentists, opticians, speech therapist, hair dresser, beauty salon. Why did you go there? What did you do there? What was it like? How did you feel?

Sam's mom had to write this formal letter. Look at the way it is formatted. Look at the punctuation and capital letters.

---

23 Fairholme Avenue,
Rushford

November 29, 2015

Mrs. Smith,
Rushford Elementary School.
Rushord

Dear Mrs. Smith,

Sam woke up feeling unwell. He had a bad headache and was hot and shivery.

I took him to the doctor who said he must stay at home for a few days. He has given him some throat lozenges to suck.

He will return to school on Monday.

Yours Sincerely,

Sam's Mom

Now write a formal letter for Kim's teacher.

(Look at the radio script with George and Christabelle to see informal writing.)

Write:

When I am happy I feel..
....

If I am awarded with:
- a treat
- a star
- a sticker
- a team point

I feel...

If I am rewarded for a good piece of work I feel (amazing), (terrific), (fantastic)..
....

BUT

When I'm sad I feel..
....

If I get (angry), (sad), (upset) or (moody) I feel...................................
....
....

If I throw a fit (temper) I feel..
....
....

Write down some mischievous things you've done.
....
....

What happened as a result of them? Who was angry?
....
....

How did you make it up?
....
....

Mrs. Barker gets her children to write...

"Don't ever say, 'I'm bored.' You may regret it."

"I don't want to hear you say I'm bored," says Dad, "you can help me in the garden."

"OH NO! I hate gardening."

Write the story, choosing a suitable ending for each sentence.

Paragraph 1

The autumn leaves are brilliant...

- *gold.*
- *red.*
- *yellow.*

and they

- *crackle*
- *crunch*
- *pop*

under my feet.

It's a good thing I am wearing my boots because the grass is ...

- *sodden.*
- *soaking wet.*
- *waterlogged.*
- *drenched.*

Writing a story

You need:

Characters (Who is in it?)
A setting (Where does it take place?)

Beginning – Introduce the characters, setting and plot.

Middle – Develop the plot with actions. Build up suspense.

End – Wind up the story with a suitable resolution.

and the thick mud is ...

- *oozing up my legs.*
- *seeping into my sneakers.*
- *slopping everywhere.*

It's ...

- *freezing cold.*
- *drizzling.*
- *dripping wet.*
- *damp and wet.*

Paragraph 2

I have raked the grass twice, but more leaves are ...

- *tumbling down.*
- *falling down.*
- *floating down.*

I've planted some spring bulbs for next spring, but the cat is ...

- *scrambling in the soil.*
- *scratching in the earth.*
- *digging up the plants.*

She ignores my angry words,

- *"Bad Cat!"*
- *"Go away!"*
- *"Leave that now. Shoo!"*

I've replanted the bulbs and I'm filling in the hole, but I scream ...

- *"Yuck! A wiggly worm."*
- *"Yuck! A hairy spider."*
- *"Yuck! A grotesque beetle."*

It
- *slowly crawls*
- *slithers*
- *slides*

⟶

- *over my arm*
- *on my hand*
- *into my boots*

Paragraph 3

I'm

- *running towards*
- *racing through*
- *heading for*

the back door.

"Where do you think you're going?" shouted Dad...

- *firmly.*
- *sternly.*
- *angrily.*

The door slams shut and I'm safe from...

- *my dad,*
- *creepy crawly creatures,*
- *things that lurk in the mud,*

although I have to face my mom who orders me to

- take off my boots.
- scrape the mud off my boots.
- clean the mud off the carpet.

Finally, I am...

- sitting
- laying
- relaxing   →
- playing
- viewing
- watching

- in a hot soapy bath
- under my warm blanket
- on the comfy sofa
- on my laptop
- the T.V.
- a D.V.D.

I peep gingerly out of the window, but Dad...

- shakes his fist.
- gives me an evil glare.
- mouths something I can't hear.

I'm in trouble again.

Autumn

We see leaves
Fall from the trees
In the wood.

We tread
On the leaves
That are spread
On the grass,
Under the trees
In the wood.

Red and orange leaves
Fall on our heads,
As we tread
On the leaves
That are spread
On the grass,
Under the trees
In the wood.

We feel brown
Shiny chestnuts,
The seeds of new trees,
Red and orange leaves
Fall on our heads,
As we tread
On the leaves
That are spread
On the grass,
Under the trees
In the wood.

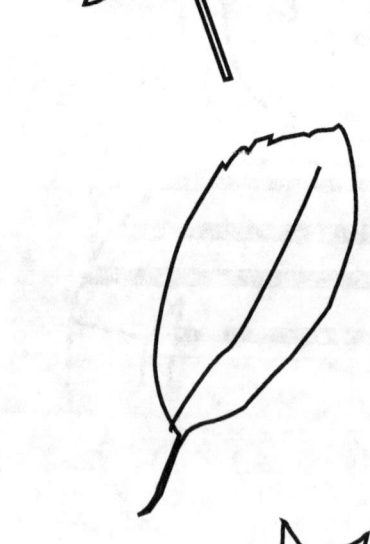

When we play
Hide and seek,
We feel
Brown shiny chestnuts,
The seeds of new trees.
Red and orange leaves
Fall on our heads,
As we tread
On the leaves
That are spread
On the grass,
Under the trees
In the wood.

Read this:

"Don't ever let me hear you say 'I'm bored' again," said Ross, my big brother. "You may regret it! Come and help me with the decorating."
"Oh no. I hate decorating!"

Now write

> Choose the best word or think up one of your own.

Paragraph 1

My older brother redecorated the living room and he made me .... (heave/hump/carry) some things up to my bedroom, so the room was empty. Soon there was such a .... (huge/enormous/massive) pile in my room that I had to .... (scramble/clamber/climb) to get to .... (the clothes in my closet/my desk/my computer). There was such a disorder that my favorite toy got .... (smashed/broken/crushed).

Paragraph 2

Then, Ross shouted, "If you've got nothing to do, you can help me .... (put dust covers over the furniture/mix and stir the paint/paint the walls)." The smell of paint was enough to make me .... (cough/splutter/choke). Ross handed me a can of orange paint and I .... (splashed/sploshed/rolled) the gooey paint onto the wall, until it dripped down with a (splodge, splish, splash). Suddenly, I heard a .... (squeal/squeak/croak) The cat/dog had brought in a .... (jumping frog/a baby bird/a tiny mouse). I .... (screamed/howled/yelled) and the paintbrush slithered out of my hand and landed on my brother's new sweatshirt that he had laid on the arm of the chair, while he went to the van to get his overalls. What a mess!

> monster is a metaphor for 'my angry brother.'

Paragraph 3

It was at that point a monster stuck its head around the door. It .... (glared/frowned/went red in the face). After this, it .... (shouted/growled/yelled) .... ("You stupid brat."/"You silly kid."/"You bad boy.") Then he said, ... ("You'll regret this"/"I'll tell Mom"/"Look what you've done") That's when I .... (stomped/stamped/groped my way) back upstairs and fought my way .... (across the assault course/through the war zone/up the treacherous rock face) that was the clutter in my bedroom, until I reached the bookcase where I chose a title, called 'Amazing Climbs.' Then I curled up on my bed, with the cat, to read my book.

Don't ever say you're bored. You might regret it.

Power Cut

A storm staggered out one night
like an evil monster looking for a fight.
It flexed its claw around our home
and spoke with a low and frightful tone.

Dad stood up at half past three
and went to the kitchen to make some tea.
Soon after that, the lights went out,
"Mom, come quick," I heard myself shout.

"I really am scared, everything's gone black.
What's happened? Are we really under attack?"
"Don't worry," she said, "there'll be light again soon.
I'll bring you a candle to brighten the room."

But at dinner time there was still no power.
The house grew colder at every hour.
We had to have bread instead of toast.
We wouldn't be cooking a nice tasty roast.

I couldn't play games or watch T.V.
There was no hot water for making more tea.
When we carefully opened the freezer door,
melted ice cream dripped all over the floor.

We ate our dinner by candlelight
and carried our candles to bed that night.
Dad said, "We'll be back to normal soon,"
so I fell asleep by the light of the moon.

Don't ever say you're bored. It might not be so bad after all.

When I arrive at the campsite on the coast, I can't wait to go to the adventure playground. I climb to the top of the jungle gym and I walk like a monkey across the bar, hanging upside down and then I go whoosh... down the slide. After this, I go so high on the tire swings that the swimming pool attendant comes over to tell me off. I do this three times and then I go back to our camping trailer. I say,
"Can we go to the beach now?" My parents are usually boiling the kettle for a cup of tea and my sister is reading a book. They always reply in the same way,
"You can't be bored already. Go and amuse yourself and give us a few minutes of peace."

On hearing this, I take my bike and ride around the campsite to see if anything has changed from last year. I prop my bike against the wall and put my head into the T.V. room, but it's full of adults watching the news. Next, I go to the campsite shop to see if they've got my favorite chewing gum, but they don't... so I stand by the little stone statue and let the cool water of the fountain trickle over my hands. I study the menu for the take-out: chicken and fries, pizza and fries and burgers and fries. I wonder what you eat if you don't like fries. Then I bike over to the washing up area and watch kids, younger than myself, fill up washing up bowls with soapy suds that overflow onto the pavement... and I watch them scrub the grease off the plates with their bony fingers. Then, I start to think about going back because I feel b..., but what was that? Suddenly, there's a big splosh on my head... then another. I'm caught in a downpour. I run for cover.

Soon I'm sitting in my trailer with Mom and Dad and my sister who's still reading. Mom is searching the trailer for a travel game of Monopoly or Scrabble. I'm pressing my nose up against the cold window and I am blowing on it so it steams up. I am watching big splashes of rain trickle down the glass, forming streams... rock pools. I imagine I'm on the beach. The dim shape of the playground is fading away under a black cloud. I want to be out there. Now, I really am bored.

Think of a vacation you have been on. Describe three things you do in detail. Use three paragraphs.

Write a story called:
Nothing's Changed

Use the plan and the sentences on the next page to help you.

1. - arrive at my trailer, it is on a campsite where I go every year
   - I go to the adventure playground, but it hasn't changed
   - ask Mom and Dad if I can go to the beach
   - They say, "You can't be bored already."

2. - ride around the campsite to explore it further
   - visit: the T.V. room
            the shop
            the fountain
            the washing up sinks
   - feel bored because nothing has changed
   - Then I feel a splash of rain. It always rains too.
   - I'm caught in a downpour and run back.

3. - sitting in the trailer
   - sister is reading a book
   - Mom is searching for a game
   - watching drips of water slide down the glass
   - wishing I could play outside
   - Now I really am bored.

(1) The first thing I do, when I arrive at my ....

is go to..

There, I climb on .... and ....

I swing on .... until ....

After this, I feel ....

so I go back to Mom and Dad and say, ".."

They reply, ".."

(2) Then I ride my bike around the..

I prop my bike against the wall and go into the T.V. room,..

the camp shop, ...

the laundry, where I ....

Next, I stand by the little stone statue and ....

Studying the menu (which has..............) I think..

By this time I start to feel b... so I think..

Suddenly, I feel a........................... then another. I'm caught in a.............................

....

(3) Soon I'm sitting in.. while my..

Mom is searching for.. and Dad is..

As I watch the big drops of rain fall ....

the playground is..

Now I wish I could... because..

....

Don't ever say you're bored. It might be better than you thought.

"We're all going to Amir's first birthday party," smiled Mom enthusiastically.
"Do we have to go?" I replied.
"You'll enjoy it," she added. As the car drove into the parking lot of the apartments where Amir's family lived, I felt bored already. I felt miserable at the thought of going to a baby's party. I couldn't even smile as we entered the backyard where a crowd of people had gathered. I handed Amir his present. He dribbled all over it. Yuck! I don't know whether he liked the present, but he certainly appreciated the wrapping paper and the bow. Could things get any worse, I thought?

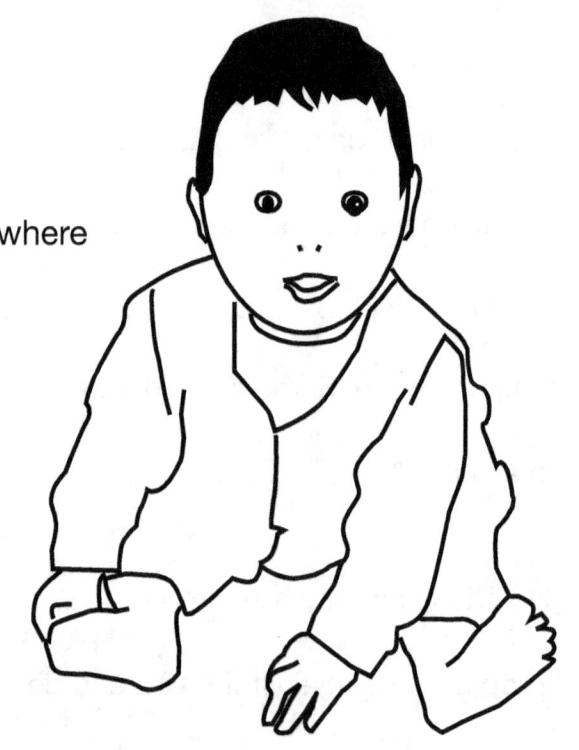

They certainly could! My mom and dad were introduced to Amir's grandparents, who came from Greece, but actually lived in Egypt. I had to stand listening to stories about what Amir had done when he visited a few months ago (eating dog biscuits from the dog's bowl). I was starting to shiver after drinking my ice cold Sprite... but then things started to get a bit more interesting. Amir's grandparents had just invited us to stay with them in Egypt, when Grandpa spied Parvitz, Amir's dad, cooking the barbecue with Amir on his shoulders and raced off to rescue him. It was at this point I was biting into my yummy lamb kebab. Suddenly, a big shaggy dog appeared around the corner and he started to eat the cocktail sausages from a plate on the table. One of the party guests fed him five more.

Now it was time to sing happy birthday to Amir. He grinned as he waited for his big moment – the blowing out of his one candle. Would he be able to do it himself I thought? His mom, Julia, helped him up to the level of the cake. We sang 'happy birthday to you, happy birthday to you, happy birthday dear Amir, happy birthday to...' At that moment, Amir stuck both his hands into the cake. He just dived into it and crammed bits of buttercream into his mouth. Most of it was smeared over his face. He chuckled at us again through the chocolate. Of course, we all had to have a piece of chocolate cake. Then it was time to say goodbye. I hugged Amir. He hugged me back.
"Thank you for inviting me to your party, little one," I said. "I loved every minute of it." "Amir is so cute," I said to my mom as we left, wiping chocolate out of my hair.

Write a story called:

The Day I Changed My Mind

Use the plan and the sentences on the next page to help you.

Characters:	Parvitz, Julia, Amir and party guests
Setting:	Flat in Rushford
Start of plot :	Amir is celebrating his first birthday but writer doesn't want to go

- gives present to Amir

....

- meets Amir's grandparents
- Parvitz cooks barbecue with Amir on his shoulder
- Grandpa rescues him
- Dog steals sausages

....

- Sing happy birthday
- Amir sticks his hands in the cake
- Smears buttercream all over his face
- Guests eat a piece of cake
- Leave and hug Amir
- Change mind – it was an amazing party

Mom said, "We're going to..."

"Do we have to.."

She replied, "You'll.."

I felt miserable because..

When I gave Amir his present, he liked the .... best.

I thought, "..."

My mom and dad were introduced to..

who said, "..

After this, the party started to get more interesting...

First Parvitz cooked the barbecue with..

Grandpa raced over to..

Then a dog appeared from nowhere and..

Now it was time for us to sing..

Amir grinned..

I wondered if he would be able to..

Then he stuck both hands in .... and ....

Of course, we all ate ....

At the end of the party I hugged .... and said, "............................"

"Amir is cute, I have changed my mind," I told my mom.

Think of a **FAMILY EVENT** you have been to.

My event

Plan

Write:

- Where did I go?
- When?
- Who was there?
- Why?
- What was the weather like?
- How did I get there?

- When I arrived ……………………
  ……………………………………
- I said, "……………………………
  ……………………………………"

....

- What happened there?
- After this…?
- Was there a problem?

- After this ……………………
- Next ……………………………
- Then ……………………………

....

- In the end, how was the problem solved?
- What did I think as I left?

- Finally ……………………………
- I thought ………………………

Write the story in three paragraphs.

Guinea Pig Education **can help you use punctuation** in *your* writing.

Let's get going!

First, don't forget to **write in sentences**. Use **capital letters** and **periods**.

Jules belongs to **S**ydney at 12 **O**live **G**rove, **R**ushford.

Now try this one:

lois and lulu belong to anya at 14 chesterfield gardens rushford

Use a **!**

That's exciting!
What a surprise!
Oh bother!

Use a **?**

What do guinea pigs eat?

Hold out a piece of vegetable. Will your guinea pig eat it?

Now try this one:

guinea pigs like to be stroked do they bite they are timid but rarely bite ouch

Do not forget to use "**.....**" when you use **direct speech**.

"Anya, what did you buy at the pet shop?" said Jules.
"I bought a cage, some straw, some hay, a bowl, a water bottle and some food for my new guinea pigs."

Use commas for **Lists**.

Use commas **before or after** a **phrase** or subordinate **clause** in a sentence.

Use commas **around a clause hidden** in the **middle of a complex sentence**.

Try these:

Lois is lively inquisitive and nosy

Guinea pigs can be chocolate black silver white and tortoise shell.

My guinea pig called Jules has long hair.

After cleaning the cage Anya put in some hay.

Try these: *(answers on next page)*

What is your guinea pig like anya

Lulu has a white coat, uneven colored spots and black ears she replied

After running in the grass Jules dozed in his hutch.

Guinea Pigs in the wild live in a burrow.

Some guinea pigs with long hair have rosettes.

Let's remember **apostrophes**:

> The carrot belonging to Jules is <u>**Jules's carrot.**</u>

> The hutch of Lois and Lulu is the **guinea pigs' hutch.**

Plus, remember apostrophes for shortened words.

> They are gorgeous.
> **They're** gorgeous.

For extra information you may need to use a **dash** for a longer pause.

> Dad bought Anya a guinea pig - it was so sweet.

> Jules nibbled his carrot loudly - crunch, crunch, crunch.

Or you could use **parentheses** for extra information.

> The guinea pigs (Lois and Lulu) scampered across the grass.

Try these:

> The guinea pig belongs to Kate.

> The hutch of the rabbits George and Ginger.

> Isnt he sweet.

Try these:

> Anya fed her guinea pig he was hungry.

> The rabbits George and Ginger are great friends.

How did you do?

- Lois and Lulu belong to Anya at 14 Chesterfield Gardens, Rushford.
- Guinea pigs like to be stroked. Do they bite? They are timid but rarely bite. Ouch!
- Lois is lively, inquisitive and nosy.
- Guinea pigs can be chocolate, black, silver, white and tortoise shell.
- My guinea pig, called Jules, has long hair.
- After cleaning the cage, Anya put in some hay.
- "What is your guinea pig like Anya?"
  "Lulu has a white coat, uneven colored spots and black ears," she replied.
- After running in the grass, Jules dozed in his hutch.
- Guinea pigs, in the wild, live in a burrow.
- Some guinea pigs, with long hair, have rosettes.
- Kate's guinea pig/ the rabbits' hutch/ Isn't he sweet.
- Anya fed her guinea pig - he was hungry.
- The rabbits (George and Ginger) are great friends.
- The male guinea pig is a boar; the female is a sow.

Finally, you can use a **colon** in a list.

> Jess had five smart guinea pigs: a short haired coat, a long coarse coat, a deep shining coat, a smooth coat and one with rosettes and twirls.

Or you can use a **semicolon** to separate two similar ideas in a list.

> Guinea pigs are sociable; they like company.

Try this:
The male guinea pig is a boar the female is a sow.

Make a sentence with a :
Make a sentence with a ;

Aren't I sweet?

Of course!

Guinea Pig **Spelling** *Tips*

Guinea pig says, "Don't forget it is important to read through your writing, so you can spot any obvious mistakes. Here are a few basic spelling tips. Make sure you can spell all the words on these pages."

Tricky homophones

Homophones sound the same but are spelled differently.

*I gave **two** carrots **to** Jules but he's getting **too** fat.*

***Our** guinea pigs **are** cute.*

*They're over **there** by **their** hutch.*

Difficult Endings

Some words have tricky endings.

*The **latch** on Jules's **hutch** comes open. He gets out and eats a **patch** of grass by the **hedge**. I try to **catch** him but he **dodges** me and runs off.*

*When I **handle** my little piggy, I **cuddle** him.*

Some words have spelling rules.

You double the final letter of a verb with a short sound.

*I **hug** Jules.
I am **hugging** him.*

*I **pat** the rabbit.
I am **patting** him.*

*I **grab** him.
I am **grabbing** hold of him.*

*He **hops**.
He is **hopping**.*

If the final letter is a consonant, just add the ending.

*He **licks**.
He is **licking**.*

*He **fights**.
He is **fighting**.*

*I **hold** him.
I am **holding** him.*

Drop the 'e' if you are adding an ending with a vowel.

*I **love** my guinea pig.
I am **loving** him.*

*I **stroke** my guinea pig.
I am **stroking** him.*

*He is having an **adventure**.
He is **adventurous**.*

Use the same rule for:

shine   shiny
noise   noisy

But, if the ending begins with a consonant you keep the 'e':

live   lively

love   lovely

lone   lonely

safe   safely

When you add an ending some words change the 'y' to an 'i':

*My guinea pig is **happy**.
He is **happier**.
He is the **happiest**.*

busy   busier   busiest
cry   cries   cried
piggy   piggies
carry   carries   carried

	Comparative	Superlative
He is fast.	faster	the fastest
He is fine.	finer	the finest
He is a beauty.	more beautiful	most beautiful

Use Sounds

ch, sh, wh, th, oo, ee, ar, or, ur, ir, er, e, ai, ay, oi, oy, oa, ow, ou, au, aw, ce, ci, cy, ge, gi, gy, short y, long y, magic e...

... to sound out 80% of words.

Use syllables to sound out hard words.

Eat **VEG** **ET** **ABLES**

Soft 'g' - ge, gi, gy.

are **COM** **FORT** **ABLE**

like **MIX** **TURE**

have an **AD** **VEN** **TURE**

SEV **EN**

PRECIOUS

CREATURE

Remember:

1. Sound hard words out using syllables.

2. Jot down words you find difficult. Learn them.

3. Use a dictionary or thesaurus.

Don't forget to keep your writing neat. Small letters should be the same height. There should be one little finger space between each word.

Make sure you can write this passage:

My guinea pigs feed on green leaves. They munch, crunch, scratch, scrunch in their hutch. Early in the morning it is necessary to feed them healthy food and fill up the water container. My noisy young pigs enjoy playing excitedly in their run on the lawn, where they are safe from danger.

Really tricky ones:

'i' before 'e' except after 'c' - when the sound is ee.

believe

fierce

field

conceited

Exceptions:

neighbor

Silent Letters:

Guinea Pigs:

gnaw

clim**b**

eat crum**b**s

are caut**i**ous

are ca**l**m

are **k**nowing

wrinkle up their noses

Tricky words:

Are you **tough enough** to keep a guinea pig?

They can't be **caught**.

They fill one with **laughter**.

They love to be **photographed**.

Guinea pig says, "Make lists of tricky words you find difficult from the groups of words."

The glossary

A starting point: is something that gives you an idea to write a story.

The genre is: the type of story you choose to write. It could be a traditional tale that has a message that good overcomes evil or a romance, horror, fantasy, mystery, realistic or adventure story.

Planning a story: Structuring the story into three or more paragraphs – with a beginning, a middle and an ending.

Characters: are people who feature in the story – we learn how they behave and about their feelings, motives, emotions and conflicts.

A setting: is the place where the story takes place - creating a mood.

The Plot: is a sequence of events that make up the story. Action in the story may be triggered by a conflict, complication, problem, or unexpected event that needs to be solved.

Suspense: is built up to leave the reader guessing what will happen. Use:
- short sentences for impact – 'Help!'
- show the feelings of the characters – 'suddenly his heart missed a beat' – to build up a dramatic climax that leaves the reader on the edge of his chair wondering how it will end.

First person: tells the story, using 'I' or 'we' – so the reader can imagine being the main character.

Second person: uses 'you' and speaks directly to the reader or involves the reader.

Third person: uses 'he,' 'she,' 'it,' 'they' to tell the story as a narrator, like a fly on the wall watching.

Atmosphere: is the mood and feeling conjured up in the story.

Flashback: if you start your story with action, you may include a few details about what went on before.

Ending or resolution: may be happy, sad, moral (a lesson learned) or a cliffhanger - where the reader imagines his or her own ending.

Paragraphs:	start a new line (one finger space in for handwriting). Use a new paragraph if you change event, time or place.
Conjunctions:	are linking words that start paragraphs or join sentences. Examples are: as, since, because, but, if, then, so, as a result of, for instance, yet, after a while, suddenly.
Dialogue:	is what people say and can move the story on. Use correct punctuation – *Lilly said, "Is it hot in here?"* (**direct speech**); *Lilly said that it was hot in here.* (**indirect or reported speech**)
The opening:	is the first sentence of a story - fiction or narrative.
A topic sentence:	is the first sentence in a paragraph, which tells the reader what it will be about. Further sentences will develop the idea and explain it.
Describe:	is making a word picture.
Adjective and noun:	*shimmering sand* (**describing word, naming word**)
Verb and adverb:	*shouting noisily* (**action word, describes action word**)
Powerful verbs and adverbs:	Choosing key words – *'a voice sounded mysteriously,' 'he nodded his head anxiously.'*
Similes:	compare using as and like – *'as white as snow'*
Metaphors:	compare two similar things, but don't use like or as. *'The dog was a little monster.'*
Script:	tells a story through the characters' dialogue.
Writers' techniques	include: 　* repetition 　* rhetorical questions - questions that don't need an answer 　* personification - giving an object human qualities 　* onomatopoeia - words that sound like their name 　* alliteration - several words that start with the same letter
Fiction:	includes story and narrative.
Non-fiction:	includes information, diaries, leaflets, reports, recounts, descriptions.
Purpose:	why it is written – to inform, explain, describe, persuade, advise or argue.
Target audience:	are the people the article is written for – to instruct someone on how to use a ..., to explain how to get somewhere, to persuade or convince the reader to do something.

www.ingramcontent.com/pod-product-compliance
Lightning Source LLC
Chambersburg PA
CBHW050715090526
44587CB00019B/3383